EVERYDAY

Artifacts:

America 1750-1850

Anthony L. Tafel

Schiffer Publishing Ltd

4880 Lower Valley Road · Atglen, PA · 19310

Other Schiffer Books on Related Subjects
American Stonewares Revised 4th Edition: The Art and Craft of Utilitarian Potters. Georgeanna H. Greer. ISBN: 0764322478. $49.95
The Brass Book, American, English, and European: 15th Century to 1850. Peter, Nancy, and Herbert Schiffer. ISBN: 091683817X. $60.00

Schiffer Books are available at special discounts for bulk purchases for sales promotions or premiums. Special editions, including personalized covers, corporate imprints, and excerpts can be created in large quantities for special needs. For more information contact the publisher:

Published by Schiffer Publishing Ltd.
4880 Lower Valley Road
Atglen, PA 19310
Phone: (610) 593-1777; Fax: (610) 593-2002
E-mail: Info@schifferbooks.com

For the largest selection of fine reference books on this and related subjects, please visit our web site at **www.schifferbooks.com**
We are always looking for people to write books on new and related subjects. If you have an idea for a book please contact us at the above address.

This book may be purchased from the publisher.
Include $5.00 for shipping.
Please try your bookstore first.
You may write for a free catalog.

In Europe, Schiffer books are distributed by
Bushwood Books
6 Marksbury Ave.
Kew Gardens
Surrey TW9 4JF England
Phone: 44 (0) 20 8392 8585; Fax: 44 (0) 20 8392 9876
E-mail: info@bushwoodbooks.co.uk
Website: www.bushwoodbooks.co.uk

Copyright © 2009 by Anthony L. Tafel
Library of Congress Control Number: 2009928011

Designed by RoS
Type set in John Handy LET/New Baskerville BT

ISBN: 978-0-7643-3361-3

Printed in China

Contents

Foreword 5

Introduction

CHAPTER 1: The First Years in America 6

CHAPTER 2: Building the House of Logs 22

CHAPTER 3: Settling In With Comfort 34

CHAPTER 4: The Farm 50

CHAPTER 5: Transportation and the Conestoga Wagon 66

CHAPTER 6: The Blacksmith 74

CHAPTER 7: The Cabinetmaker 88

CHAPTER 8: Hodgepodge 98

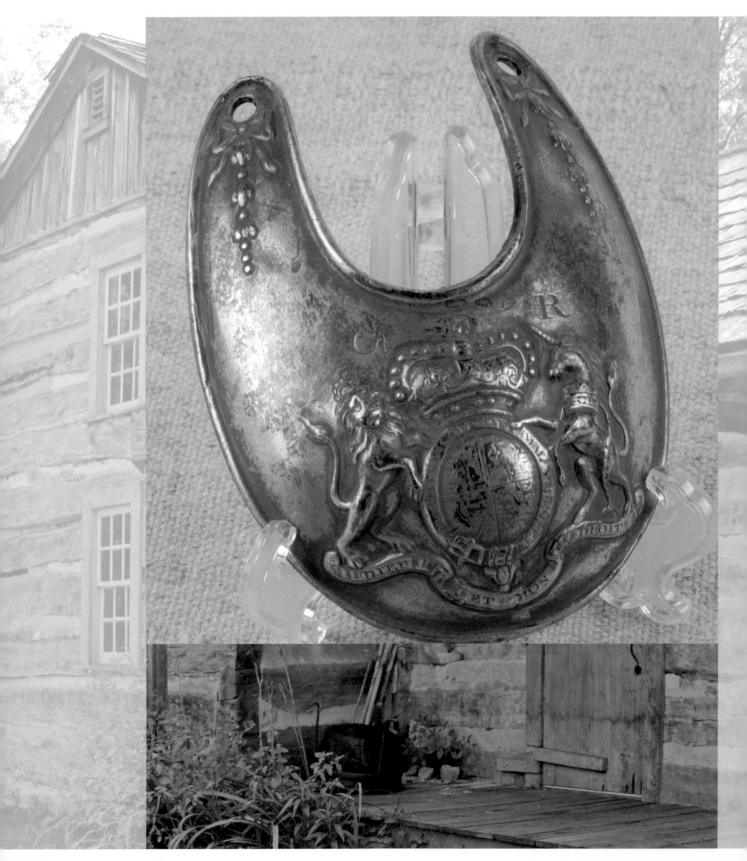

Foreword

From what I can see there are two types of collectors. The first type of collector purchases an item for the collection, but the collection is seldom seen or shared in any way because the collection is "boxed" away.

The second type of collector acquires items for the collection but the pieces collected are not boxed away. They are shown and shared with anybody who has even the slightest interest. One of our moves caused me to box up my Civil War collection. After settling into the new house I realized there was no space to display my collection. The items stayed boxed for a few months in the attic before I realized that because they were out of sight, and therefore of no use, I needed to sell them. Away they went.

After moving again, I began to collect antique tools and anything relating to the life of the average American between 1750 and 1850. This book – and the high quality photographs available from the publishing company – enables me to share my collection with you. I couldn't ask for anything more, and I hope you have as much fun with the book as I did putting it together.

I would like to add special thanks to my wife, Ruth, for her help in putting this book together.

Introduction

The reason for writing this book is to create an interesting and enjoyable opportunity to examine the artifacts that our ancestors used in settling this country more than two hundred and fifty years ago. If you are a collector, or simply someone interested in American history, this information will be of interest. Many books about the history of the early years of the country do not have good photographs that support the information given in the book. With this book, the photographs are the story.

If your interest is from the collector's point of view, you will find many early tools described. The tools of the blacksmith, cabinet-maker, carpenter, and farmer are discussed, along with the more general tools brought to these shores by the first colonists. If your interest is early Americana, you will find many personal items pertaining to the everyday life of these brave adventurers. Some of the artifacts illustrated may be new to the reader, and if this is so, this project will have been a success. As a teacher, I believe that learning should be enjoyable. Have fun with this book and if something new is learned, be sure to share it with a friend.

CHAPTER 1
The First Years in America

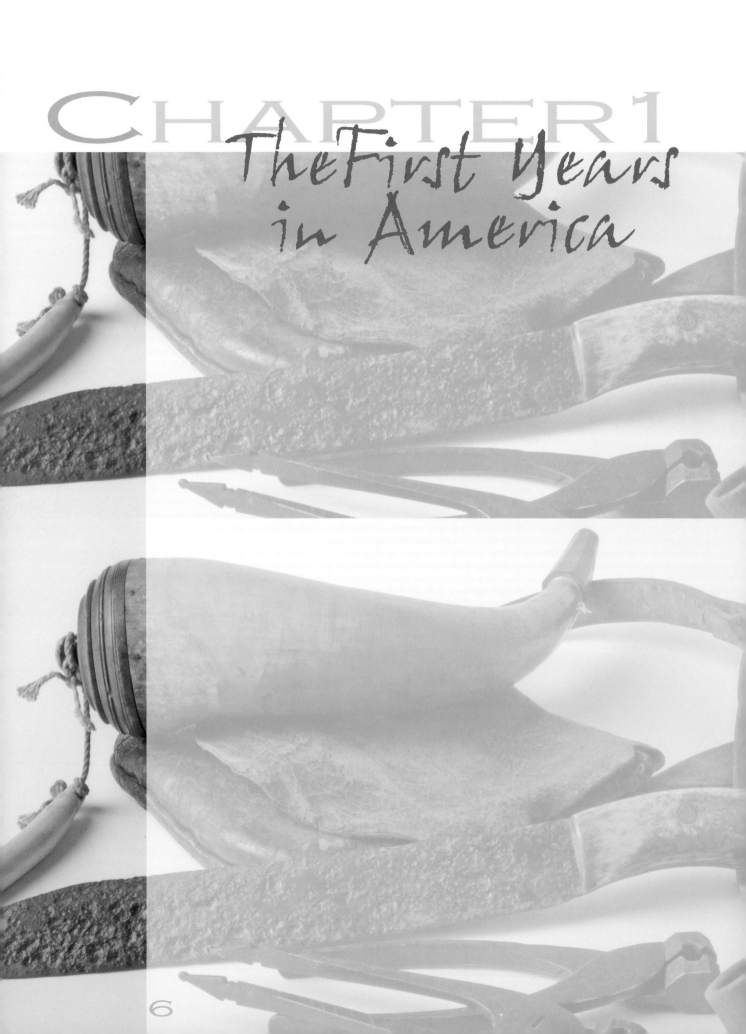

When the colonists arrived in America they found a land of forests. Since it appeared this land was never ending woods, the felling axe and hatchet became the primary tools for development. The axe cleared the forest, the surveyor's chain laid out the plots, the long rifle gave protection and food, and the horse and oxen supplied power and transportation.

Along with these tools, the early colonists brought with them other items such as newspapers, farming tools, knives, and clothing styles, just to mention a few. Once on these shores, their prime mission was to obtain freedom from danger as quickly as possible. They worked long hours to clear enough land to build a log house, develop a small vegetable garden, and raise enough meat to feed the family. These men and women were made of hardy stock with a will to survive the harsh conditions found in their adopted new land. Without this drive and determination, early colonists might not have been able to survive and grow into what we know as America.

The following photographs illustrate some of the artifacts used by these men and women as they forged a new life in a new land.

The London Gazette.

Numb. 1027

Published by Authority.

From Monday September 20. to Thursday September 23. 1675.

Venice, Sept. 7.

Here are arrived two Vessels from *Smirna*, by whom we have advice, That the Plague rages very much in several parts of *Turky*, and that they continue to assemble all the Forces they can, to send them against *Poland*. And by another Vessel come from *Ganea*, we have an account, That 14 Turkish Gallies were arrived there to take in Soldiers, to be likewise employed against the *Poles*; so that it seems, the Grand Signior is resolved to carry on this War with all the Force he is able; and the rather, for that he understands the *Poles* are in an ill condition, and seems to expect that the approach of his Armies will oblige them to make peace upon such terms as he shall think fit to prescribe.

Copenhagen, Sept. 17. Yesterday sailed from hence the Sieur *Rooyseen*, with a Squadron of Men of War towards *Gottenburg*, to free the Sea of the Swedish Capers on that side. Our Fleet takes several prizes in the Baltique, which are daily sent up h ther. We are assured that his Majesty will continue with the Army, as long as there seems to be any appearance of Action.

Vienna, Sept. 11. This day is arrived here a Gentleman dispatched by the Marquis *deGrana*, to give his Imperial Majesty an account of the reduction of *Treves*. The Troops march still towards *Egra* in *Bohemia*, where we hope to hear ere long that they are come together in a Body; some have reported that General *Souches* is to command them, but without any certainty. Several endeavors are still used to persuade the Elector of *Bavaria* to embrace the party of the Emperor, and the Confederates, but his Electoral Highness persists in his resolution to keep a Neutrality; though it is reported, that two D puties are come from his Electoral Highness to treat with the Ministers of this Court on that Subject. A party of Turks of the Garison of *Newhausel*, have lately fallen into the Countrey of *Nitria*, committed many disorders there, and burnt a Village down to the ground; of which the Imperialists at *Raab* being advertised, sent out a party of *Hussars*, who overtook the Turks ere they got to their Garison, killed most of them, and redeemed above 30 Christians, whom they had made slaves and were carrying away with them. From *Hungary* we are told, that some of the Rebels have of late committed many disorders.

Hamburgh, Sept. 24. The French and Swedish Ministers are at length departed from hence. Since the Conference that was held at *Gadebusch*, the Danish and Brandenburg Armies are on their march towards *Pomeren*; the 21 instant, the King of *Denmark* had his quarters not far from *Wismar*, where he resolved to remain two days to refresh his Soldiers, and then to continue his march. The Dutch and Danish Men of War which cruise in the Baltique, have as we are told, t ken several prizes since their being abroad, and on the 19 instant, they at one time took twelve or thir-

teen Vessels with a small Man of War that convoyed them. The Bishop of *Munster* meets with difficulty to pass his Forces over the *Weser*, the *Suedes* disputing their passage. The Duke of *Luxenburg Zell* is arrived at *Zell*.

Bremen, Sept. 18. The Deputies which came hither from the Bishop of *Munster*, having delivered their Message to our Magistrates, concerning the passage which the Bishop desired for his Forces over our Bridge, and received their answer; which, we are told, in substance was, That they could not permit the said passage: on Monday they returned to *Wilshusen*, where the Bishop at present is with the Danish General *Baudies*; who, the 16, after that a Council of War had been held in the presence of the Bishop, came on the South-side of this place, under our Cannon, to view, as ti believed, how their Troops might best pass the *Weser*. This morning we have heard much shooting; and the Boors that come to Town tell us, that the *Suedes* have planted four pieces of Cannon on this side of the River, to oppose the passage of the *Munsters*, who have likewise brought their Cannon on the other side, to favor the same.

Ditto, Sept. 23. Hitherto the Munster Troops remain on the other side of the *Weser*, their passage being opposed by the Suedes, who stand on this side with several pieces of Cannon; the Count *de Horne* hath sent them a reinforcement of 1000 Musqueteers, so that it's thought, the Munsters will find great difficulty to get over the River, and therefore the Bishop with so much the more earnestness solicites our Magistrates to grant them passage over our Bridge.

Strasburgh, Sept. 18. The 12 instant, the Right Wing of the Imperial Army, under the command of the Marquis of *Baden*, begun the siege of *Saverne*, while the Left took care of the Convoy that went from hence; the 13 and 14, the Marquis de *Baden* battered the Town very furiously, and they within answered him in the same kind; but receiving orders from General *Monte usuli*, (who the 13 received two Couriers with Letters from *Vienna*) on the 15, early in the morning, the Marquis marched off with his Troops from before *Saverne*, with so much haste, that in less than two hours they had all left their Posts which they had before the place; and having joined the Left Wing, the whole Army marched towards *Pfiffenhouen*, which is about two Leagues from *Haguenaw*. In the mean time we are altogether uncertain what *Montecuculi's* design is; some say, That he will march directly into *Lorraine*; but others tells us, That he will besiege *Pitspburgh*; and we rather believe the latter, for that the Cannon that were sent from hence to the Army, are carried down the *Rhine* to *Stolhoffen*; and that it is ordered that all Provisions that go from hence to the Army, shall pass down the *Rhine*.

Treves, Sept. 16. We are at present busied here about repairing the Fortifications, and putting this place into a posture of defence. Some days since came hither five or six French Soldiers from *Metz*, who had deserted; they all assure us, That the French are assembling a Body of an Army about *Verdun*, for the reinforcement of the Prince

---

Many of the early settlers would bring familiar items with them when they made the long voyage to America. This 1675 newspaper is an example of such an item. 6.75" x 10".

Tripod, probably early nineteenth century. A telescope would be set into the circular brass band.

Land was surveyed and purchased. This survey done in 1740 was signed by Thomas Penn, son of William Penn. 7" x 12".

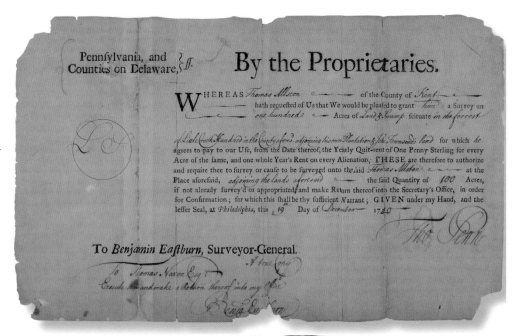

Another survey, this one signed in 1765 by John Penn, another son of William Penn. 8" x 12.5".

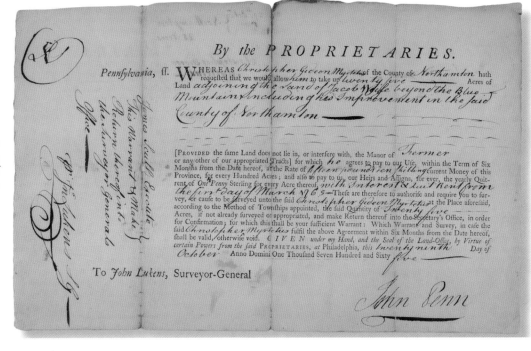

An eighteenth century telescope, the type that could be set into a tripod and used for surveying. It measures 27" when fully opened.

Once land was purchased in the New World, brush had to be cleared and fences set. Pictured is a common Bill Hook for clearing brush along with a Gunter's Chain for surveying. This chain is sixty-six feet long, and was invented by Edmund Gunter, an English mathematician, in 1620. To use this chain one man held the chain at each end and stretched it out straight. Eight chain lengths equaled one mile; ten square chains equaled one acre; a canal way is the width of one chain; three chains equaled a city block, and one chain is the width of a street. A fence rail is generally eleven feet in length, one sixth of a chain.

Conventional wood banded canteen, used by early settlers while working in the field, setting fences, felling trees or clearing brush. This canteen measures 9" in diameter.

Every early settler had his long rifle or musket. This weapon has a flintlock mechanism, curly maple stock, and is considered a common fowling piece of the time. It was, most likely, made in England.

Two gunpowder containers. The smaller barrel could be carried easily since it is only 4" high and 5" in diameter. The larger barrel was purchased from the powder manufacturer and measures 10" in diameter and 14" high.

Items the early settlers could not do without include a powder horn with the gunpowder inside, powder measure made out of bone, hunting bag, bullet molds, and side knife.

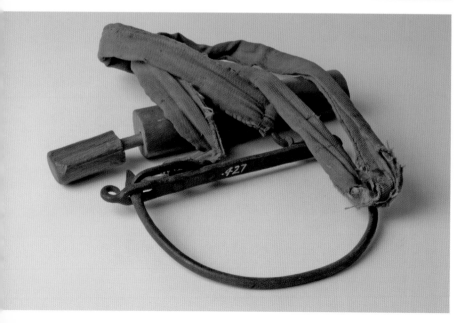

Above:
The pocket knife was a very important item. Pocketknives came is all sizes and all shapes, some with bone handles, some with wood handles. These are all eighteenth or early nineteenth century examples.

Animal traps were important to the settling of the land. This hand-forged trap has the punched in date of 1832.

Among the equipment early hunters would carry with them are the game hook, used to carry rabbits and other small game that had been taken, and the turkey call. Both of these items are eighteenth or early nineteenth century artifacts.

The striker and its flint were used to start the fire. This striker with the original leather pouch for holding tinder and the "penny" knife are artifacts of the eighteenth and early nineteenth centuries.

A grouping of early strikers showing the many shapes in which they were made. Most of these were excavated in New York State.

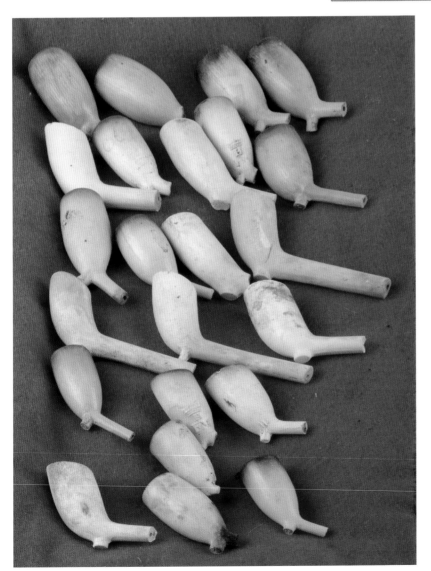

A group of eighteenth century pipe tampers. The one in the center is found on the end of a very early spoon.

Clay pipes recovered from the Philadelphia waterfront in the early 1960s, dating from the sixteenth through the eighteenth century. Note the many different shapes

The first years in America found many styles of canteens. This one is made of a hollowed log with two iron bands and a leather carrying strap. It measures 10" long and 7" in diameter.

Whistles were a common way of communicating during the eighteenth century. This grouping is of horn, pewter, and brass.

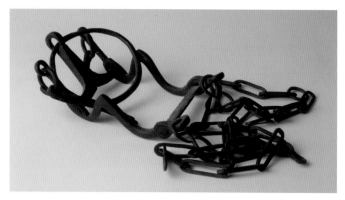

The horse was an important part of the early years in America. This ring bit is a standard type used in the eighteenth century, and it is totally blacksmith made.

A bone handled side knife, typical of many carried in the belt for hunting and self protection.

A variety of trade axes with various shapes and markings. All of these axes were made during the eighteenth and early nineteenth centuries.

A representative belt hatchet of the Revolutionary period. This style hatchet was carried by many foot soldiers during the Revolutionary War.

This eighteenth century trade axe is a relic of Lancaster County, Pennsylvania.

During the early years in America, the buttons on clothing were pewter, brass, and bone. Here is a small example of the civilian buttons in use at the time.

The beaver, broad brimmed hat was a favorite with many men of the time. This example is 5" high and 16" in diameter.

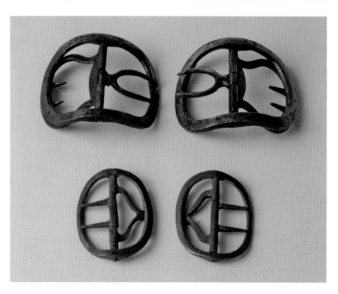

A pair of shoe buckles. Shoe buckles were the style until the early nineteenth century.

The upper pair of buckles are a child's pair of shoe buckles. The lower buckles were used on knee britches, pulling the britches tight just below the knee.

16

Because store bought items were scarce, many things had to be improvised. These three drinking cups, made of cow horn, are prime examples of what could be made and used very effectively.

A very small "pen" knife with a bone handle. This folding knife was used to sharpen the quill pen when the tip became bent or broken, thus the modern name for the penknife. This knife measures 2" in length.

Smoking and snuff were both very popular during this time. One of these snuff boxes is made of horn; the other is made from the burl of a tree.

From Top:
As mentioned earlier, the horse was essential to the early settler. These three horseshoes were forged no later than the early nineteenth century.

Pockets in clothing were not a common item in the 1700s. These three finely forged "hangers" were hung on a leather belt and items could be hung from them. Both men and women used them during that time.

Typical eyeglasses and leather wallet of the eighteenth century.

Small belt axe head with an old tag that reads, "Ancient tomahawk dug up near Salem Massachusetts, very similar to the axes used by the Pilgrim fathers."

The axe was a very important tool to the early colonists, coming in many shapes and sizes. This one has a tag that reads, "Axe head from John Alden's house at Plymouth, Mass. Taken from an excavation there about 12 years ago [1935] to a depth of 18 feet. The work was done by M. Mooney, formerly a sailor and steeple jack, now a contractor in summer at Nantucket Island, Mass."

A common felling axe used during the first years by the colonists. Marked "M SIEGER."

Every blacksmith tended to have his own design style. This is a very unique shape for a felling axe. The axe is unmarked as to maker.

A very early form for a felling axe. No maker's name.

An axe that is a transition in shape from the early trade axe styles to the more modern form of head with "ears." These ears are the triangular extensions on each side of the head along the handle that help stabilize the head to the handle.

This axe is one of the earliest patterns used in the colonies. It was this style that was also traded to the Indians. This tool was a very awkward item to use as the balance was misplaced, making the swing a difficult process to master.

Once the timber was cut down, it had to be split into manageable pieces. These forged, splitting wedges are examples that were used in early Pennsylvania. The stampeded decorations had a purpose other than, as the Germans would say, "making pretty." Stamping helped keep the wedge from jumping out of the wood when struck by the maul.

The first years in America were not always easy. With the use of the items described in this chapter, the colonists were able to clear an opening and build a structure that was suitable for their needs at the time. Real comfort would come later.

CHAPTER 2
Building the House of Logs

*E*arly settlers questioned what they could do with the vast amount of timber that they had cleared from the land. Much of the wood was burned, fence posts and rails were made, and the log cabin was built. However, the idea of building with logs in this country was not a new idea, as many settlers were familiar with the log cabin in their homeland. The first cabins were small but as time went on the buildings became larger and more sophisticated. Not all of the log houses were of the same quality. Some had logs fitting so tightly together that a finger could not be put between the logs, while others required large amounts of chinking to fill in the gaps between the logs.

The tools required to build such a dwelling were fairly basic. The felling axe, hewing axe and hatchet (for squaring the logs), auger, dividers, adz, and drawknife were all tools that most of the colonists would have had in their tool chest. It was the skill of the builder that was essential in order to use the tools effectively.

The following photographs illustrate some of the tools and artifacts needed to build the house of logs and you will see, depending on the skill of the builder, how both log cabins and log houses were built. Some of these dwellings, because of their size, are quite impressive.

Many of the early settlers would not think of building a home until they knew the directions of north, south, east, and west because they wanted to face a true direction. This eighteenth century compass is 2.5 inches square.

An example of one of the many early buildings built of logs.

A cabin in western Pennsylvania showing the typical notching system used at the corners. The axe and hatchet were the two most used tools for this work.

A very early axe used in roughing out the timbers.

This "goosewing" axe is an early design. The job of this tool was to flatten the four sides of a round log by slicing off chips. A chalk line would be followed in order that the chipping would stay straight.

Goosewing hewing axe marked H STAHLER. For the hewing axe and hewing hatchet, the cutting edge bevel is only on one side. The back side of the head is flat all the way down to the cutting edge. Because of this, the user can make a smooth cut on the side of a log.

An early form of hewing axe, a screwdriver, and bevel gauge, all tools used in cabin building.

Hewing axe of the goosewing design with a string winder, a plumb bob, and a framing square. This square is stamped with the name, I BRUMBACH 1813.

Close-up of the stamping on the "BRUMBACH" square.

Hewing axe marked HOFMAN.

Hewing axe and two race knives. When preparing to join two pieces of wood together, the race knife would be used to scribe numerals on the matching pieces so that the builder would know which two pieces fit together at what exact point.

Another shape for the hewing axe. One interesting thing about these early axes is that they were made in a variety of shapes. Every blacksmith had his style and design elements, some of them resembling works of art.

A very large hewing axe. The blade measures 15.5" wide. This pattern of axe is called the "Pennsylvania Pattern." Alongside of the axe is a "log dog." It was used to steady the log being hewn.

A nicely decorated hewing axe and an ox shoe. The ox was indispensable in building the log house because of the power it provided.

When building the house of logs, the axe was king. Other necessary tools were the strap hammer, the two-foot rule, and a keg of the beverage of the day—usually water.

Another early hewing axe, along with some reading material. The *Porcupine's Gazette*, by William Cobbett, was printed in Philadelphia, opposite Christ Church, January 1799.

The adz would smooth out the surface of a log or board. All of the carpenter's tools were kept razor sharp and because of this many a toe was removed, even with boots on, by this tool.

Other items used in log house building were the auger, for drilling holes, another strap hammer, and a nail pouch made from the top of an old discarded boot. Note the slits in the boot top for a leather belt.

The froe, with its wooden handle at right angles to the blade, would be used to split the shingles; the draw knife [1804] was used to shave the wood to a final fit. The peg cutter would make pegs, all in the same diameter, by driving the rough-cut peg through the cutter with a wooden mallet. This froe blade was forged from an old horseshoe rasp, as is evident from the teeth of the rasp still being visible.

This drawknife was made by V HOFMAN.

The eighteenth century square with its decorated end, the strap hammer, and the drawknife are all tools used for cabin construction.

This eighteenth century panel saw is unusual in that it has lead rivets used to hold the grip to the blade. With the saw are both a pair of dividers and a framing square.

Post hole axe with three markings. The earliest mark cannot be read clearly but the other two are SILVIUS, and HOFMAN.

Post hole axe with two blacksmith marks stamped V HOFMAN and G SENER. These axes were used to cut the mortises out of the beams for the log houses and for cutting the holes in fence posts for the rails.

Post hole axe with the date 1837 stamped into the pole. The pole is the iron counter-balance to the blade.

A twybill, or two billed axe. These are quite rare. They were used to chip and clean out very deep mortises.

Another hard to find tool used in the building of the log house is the deep mortising chisel axe. It was used to smooth the walls of the mortise to ensure a tight fit with the tenon.

To drill holes for pegs, the wood brace, and bit were used along with the hand auger.

Wood carving of the pit saw in use. This method of sawing boards from a log is ancient and continued through the entire eighteenth century. The boards for the cabin may have been sawn on the site or someplace else.

These three log houses in western Pennsylvania illustrate the structures that were built using the type of tools described in this chapter. They may look crude to us today, but they were home to the people who built them. Life was hard, but with time, comfort would come to the log home.

CHAPTER 3
Settling In with Comfort

When many of the early settlers arrived on these shores their belongings were very meager. Only the necessities were brought with them, although some were told by earlier arrivals that certain things were essential to bring, especially tools. With only the basics, settlement was started. Deprived of the objects that made life comfortable back home, they soon became eager to obtain these comforts as quickly as possible. Little by little, certain comforts acquired created a softening of life, but this often took years to accomplish.

The blacksmith, cabinetmaker, and merchant were a necessity. Until these tradesmen were in place, life had to be based on total self-sufficiency. Once items were available for purchase or barter, the life of the colonist became much more comfortable. Candles no longer had to be dipped, coffee could be purchased and ground, cooking could be done with many pots and utensils, books could be obtained, newspapers read, and ruffles on clothes could be ironed.

The following photographs represent many of the items that made life more comfortable to the men and women who first settled in America.

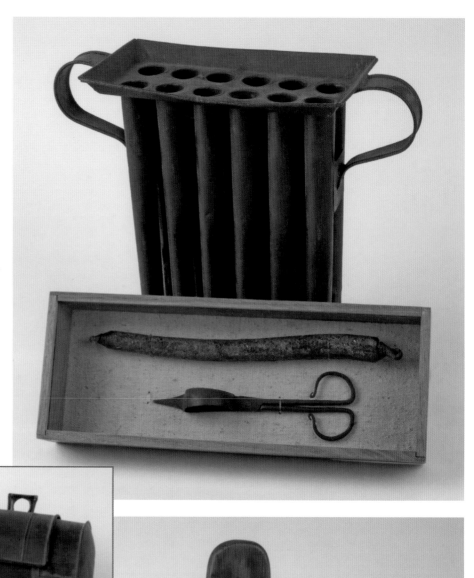

As time went on the colonist's possessions began to grow and life became easier. Early lighting consisted of rush lighting and hand dipped candles, the latter a laborious process. This twelve hole candle mold, with an original molded candle and iron snuffer, provide examples of an easier way to create light.

Tin candle box used to store the very valuable candles after they were made.

Three types of candle holders that were found in the home, typical during the eighteenth and nineteenth centuries.

Spill plane and spills. The spill was simply a long curled shaving that could be used as a match when it was ignited from an existing flame. This particular plane was made simply to create that shaving. Most planes created shavings as waste, where the spill plane made shavings as the main product. The spills made it simple to move a fire from one place to another without the danger of moving hot coals.

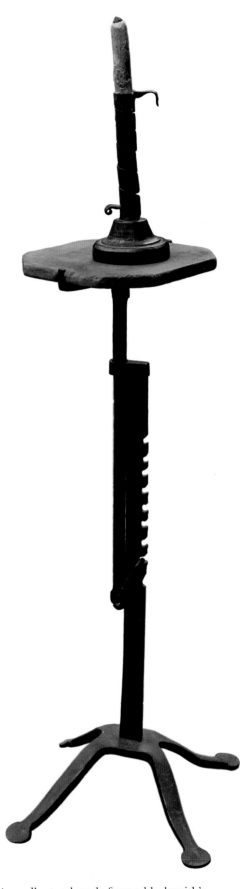

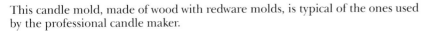

This candle mold, made of wood with redware molds, is typical of the ones used by the professional candle maker.

A candle stand made from a blacksmith's "helper." The blacksmith would have used this stand, without the wood top, to help support long pieces of bar iron as he was working with them. The small piece of wood was added later, and a candle stand was created.

Horn and wood were common materials around the homestead. The three spoons, comb, shoehorn, and salt containers are made of cow horn. One spoon is made of wood.

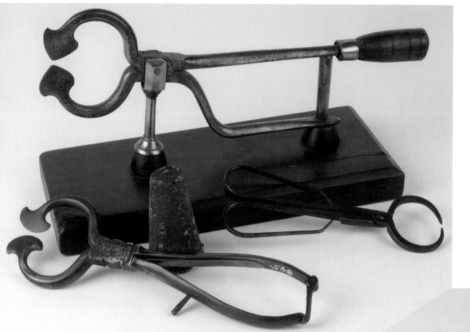

Sugar was a treat and it was used sparingly. It came to the colonists in the shape of a cone and had to be cut with special cutters called sugar nippers.

During the first years of settlement, pewter was not available, so most eating ware was made of wood. This woodenware was called treenware. The knife and fork date around 1740.

Dough cutters, or jagging wheels, were common in the kitchen. Shown with the cutters is a bowl made from the burl of a tree.

Coffee grinder, eighteenth century. This style of coffee grinder is typical of the one George Washington used at Mount Vernon.

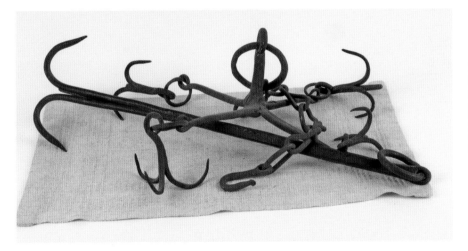

In the smokehouse there were meat hooks hanging from the beams which were used to hold the meat during the smoking process. In the kitchen there were bird hooks hanging from the ceiling, which held the latest game before it was cleaned and ready for cooking.

Treenware was slowly replaced by pewter. These pewter bowls are believed to be early nineteenth century British navy mess bowls. The spoons are typical of pieces used in the early eighteenth century.

In the kitchen, as times got better, pewter replaced wood. This large "charger," 17" in diameter, and two porringers, 5" and 4.5" in diameter respectively, are examples of items that would be found in many homes during the eighteenth century.

Time was a very important part of the lives of the early colonists. No time was to be wasted. This eighteenth century pewter hourglass is a four-minute timer. It stands 6" tall.

Detailed photo of the "wedding set" handles.

In many homes the kitchen would have had a vegetable chopper and a very ornate "wedding set" consisting of the ladle and strainer. When a couple married, it was often the custom to present the bride with an ornate set of cooking utensils. The large spoon is blacksmith made and would have been used to stir the contents of a sizable pot.

Once some comfort was setting in, among the items found in the log home would be the pantry box and the "hide-a-way" book. This book probably hid some important papers or letters, while the pantry boxes came in different sizes and held dry ingredients used in the kitchen.

Ironing, when it was done, was done with a flat iron. Ruffles would have to be ironed with the goffering iron shown here. To use this tool the iron rod was removed and heated, then inserted into the brass holder. The rod heated the brass and the ruffles were pressed over the round, heated end.

Knife and fork, c.1790, bone apple corer and bone marrow spoon. Marrow was a favorite food and to remove it from the bone would be impossible without this utensil.

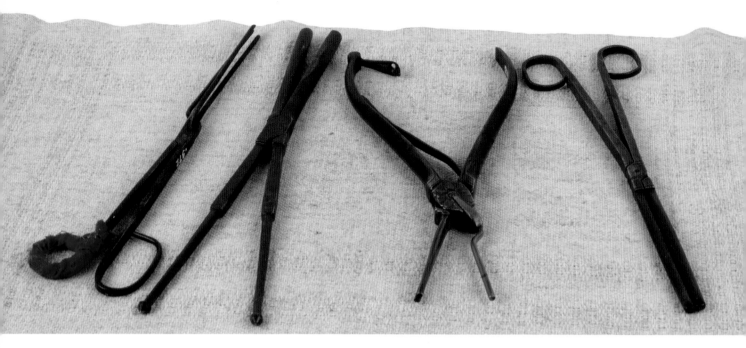

An assortment of wig curling irons. These were heated before use.

The canteen was an important part of any work outside. The beverage could have been either cider or water.

When traveling from the home, personal belongings were carried in hand bags or trunks. This small leather covered "stagecoach" trunk is lined with a newspaper dated 1822. The trunk measures 11" long, 7" high, and 6.5" deep.

Every home had a spinning wheel. To save the spinner from developing blisters, the "knocker," made of tiger maple, was used to spin the wheel.

Shaving was done with a straight razor. These four eighteenth century straight razors, as well as a shaving box for soap, are common examples.

Tin shaving bowl. The bowl was held under the chin while shaving, to catch the water and shavings.

For those who liked their drink, this leather covered shoulder flask was the perfect thing. This flask is early to mid-nineteenth century.

To warm the sheets on a cold night, a bed warmer was used. Hot coals were put into the pan and then run back and forth over the bed sheets until the desired temperature was reached.

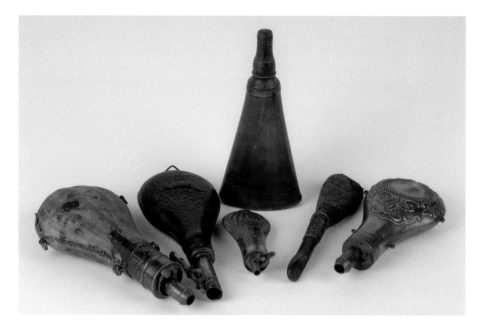

A powder horn was the old method of carrying gunpowder. Flasks were available in horn, brass, copper, and zinc. The small leather pouch carried bird shot for hunting.

When a gentleman went out for the evening, he would wear his best beaver hat. The style tells us that this hat was worn about 1840. The label inside the crown of the hat states "SHULTZ & BRO. LANCASTER, PA."

Dogs during the eighteenth century occasionally had collars. Although this collar is of English manufacture, it could very well have been used in the colonies.

Comfort could be described as reading the paper by the fire. The *General Advertiser* was printed by Benjamin Franklin Bache, grandson of Benjamin Franklin, in Philadelphia, in 1797, and the *Intelligencer, and Weekly Advertiser* was printed by William Dickerson in Lancaster, Pennsylvania, in 1808.

Fires were a constant threat to log homes in the early days of America. Fire brigades were organized by neighborhoods, and the fire bucket was their means of fighting the fire. Every home owned a bucket and the owner would bring his bucket to the fire being fought. Men would form a line from the water source to the fire, each man with a bucket. A bucket full of water would be passed up the line, and at the end of the line the water in the bucket would be thrown on the fire. Then the empty bucket would be sent back down the line. This process would be repeated over and over again until the fire was under control.

Letter writing was important, and there were certain items that made the task possible. On the desk would be the pewter writing set containing the ink (ink containers missing), the sander, and quill pen. Also shown is a wooden sander holding the blotting sand, and the wax jack. This jack held the wax that was melted onto the folded letter, after which the seal was pushed into the hot wax, leaving the owner's mark.

Many homes surrounded their fireplaces with tiles. The tiles pictured here range in age from the early 1600s through the mid-1700s. They are considered delftware but not all tiles were made in the Netherlands at Delft. These tiles were most likely manufactured in England at one of their delftware factories. They are 5/16" thick with the four larger ones measuring 5" square and the smaller one measuring 3.25" square.

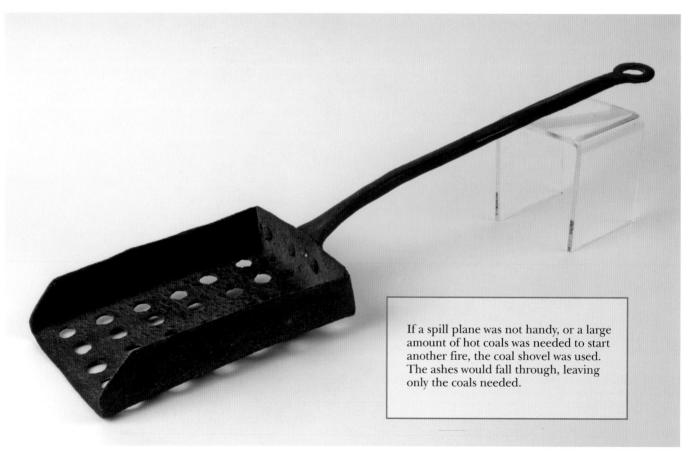

If a spill plane was not handy, or a large amount of hot coals was needed to start another fire, the coal shovel was used. The ashes would fall through, leaving only the coals needed.

The foot warmer is another item of comfort that required hot coals. It was used to warm toes while in the carriage, in church, or anyplace that a cold draft could be found.

Life centered around the hearth. The bellows and tongs kept the fire going, while pipe tongs kept the pipe lit and the landholder content.

The fireplace was the most important part of the home. Without it there would be no heat for comfort or cooking. Two utensils important to the fireplace were the shovel to move ashes, and the fork to adjust the logs. This distinctive fork handle is made from an old flintlock gun barrel. The handle of the shovel has a very unique, hand-forged knob.

47

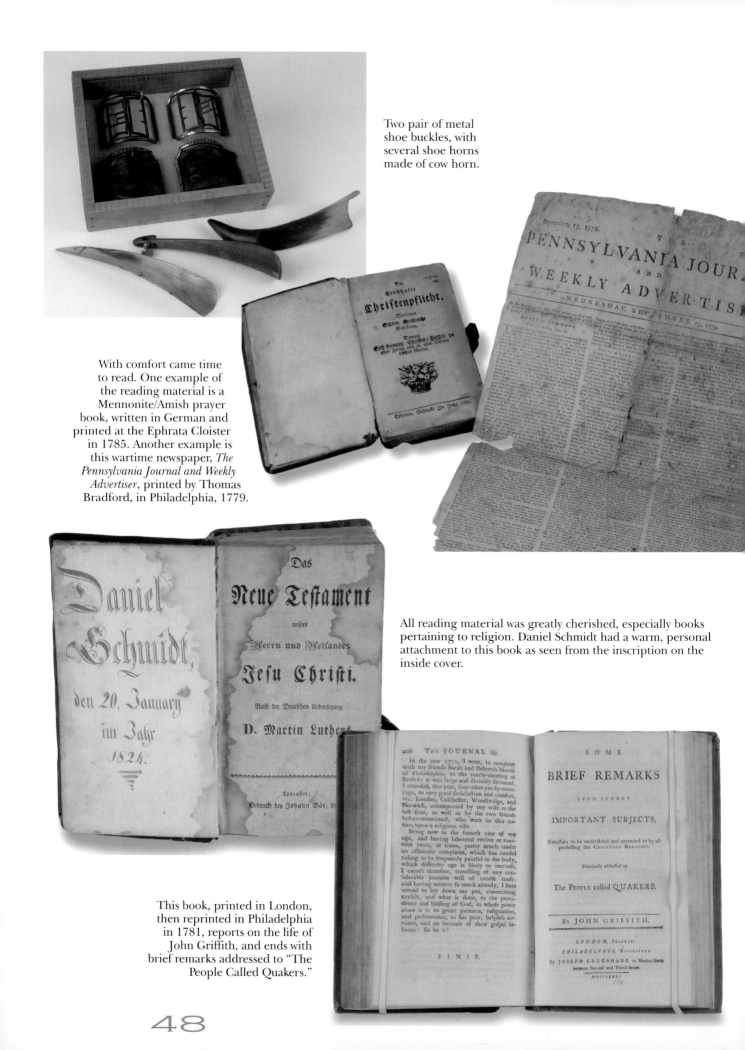

Two pair of metal shoe buckles, with several shoe horns made of cow horn.

With comfort came time to read. One example of the reading material is a Mennonite/Amish prayer book, written in German and printed at the Ephrata Cloister in 1785. Another example is this wartime newspaper, *The Pennsylvania Journal and Weekly Advertiser*, printed by Thomas Bradford, in Philadelphia, 1779.

All reading material was greatly cherished, especially books pertaining to religion. Daniel Schmidt had a warm, personal attachment to this book as seen from the inscription on the inside cover.

This book, printed in London, then reprinted in Philadelphia in 1781, reports on the life of John Griffith, and ends with brief remarks addressed to "The People Called Quakers."

All of the children had handmade toys, and they loved them.

Adults often entertained themselves with lawn bowling either on a green, or as close as they could come to a flat, grassy surface. This lawn bowling ball measures 6" in diameter and is believed to be made of lignum vitae. It weighs eight pounds.

A show towel, plain but interesting. Made by the woman of the house, these were hung on the backs of doors to brighten up the room. The material is homespun linen, and cross-stitched into the towel,

CHAPTER 4
The Farm

Because it was essential for the early colonists to be self-sufficient, it was a natural process for them to become farmers. The farm could be a simple cabin and barn of logs, or, as time progressed, a grander house and barn of stone. Whether you were a blacksmith, a cabinetmaker, or a shoemaker, you most likely grew up as a farmer, if for no other reason than survival.

These men and women had calluses on their hands, and no one was afraid of long hours of hard manual labor. The tools and skills the farmer possessed were enormous. Swinging an axe and managing a plow were daily chores. They knew how to make apple cider. They knew how to make butter and cheese and ham. They knew animals and how to use them. They knew the growing seasons and what to plant. And aside from doing all of the daily chores, the farmer was often asked to be a soldier. Their work lasted from before sun-up to after sundown, day after day. The philosophy of "hard work reaps rewards" came naturally to the men and women living in those early years, but for us living today it is a value many have lost.

The farmer of long ago has left many reminders of his existence, as numerous old farm tools and artifacts can be found in antique shops and auction houses around the country. This chapter illustrates some of the more unique artifacts left to us by those ancestors living during the eighteenth and early nineteenth centuries.

A farmer's day book dated 1793. Some
of the listings are, "mendon a plow, half day
planton, oxen half day to plowen, half day at barn, to killen calf, to
half day raken, oxen half day to draw hay, to mendon shoes 2 pair".

Iron banded canteen used while in the field with
measurements 11" in diameter and 6.5" deep.

Whetstone
horns used to
hold the sharpening
stone for the sickles and scythes.
These were attached to the user's waist belt so
that the whetstone was always handy when needed.
Horn can be shaped by heating in hot oil, then while still
hot, molded. When cooled it was just as hard as it was before. It could
be carved, reshaped, and even turned on the lathe.

A decorated whetstone horn. These designs are typical of Pennsylvania German designs.

Another view of the same horn.

Horns were often personalized. "Ben: B: 1843" was carved into this horn.

Another view of the same horn.

To bring the cutting edge back to the proper sharpness on the sickle or scythe blade, a denglesteck, or small anvil, was used with a small hammer. The anvil (denglesteck) was hammered into a stump with the small flat surface on top. The edge of the blade to be sharpened was set on the top of the anvil and the cutting edge was lightly hammered. This process was done many times in a day's work to keep the tool sharp.

Grease horns were used as containers for the grease needed to lubricate the wagon axles. The horns were hung under the wagon so that they were handy when needed. This set of ox horns, with each horn measuring 30" long, is unusual because of their size.

Hand forged garden rake. The blacksmith made this rake sometime from the mid- to late eighteenth century.

Two styles of pitchfork. Both are hand-forged and date to the late eighteenth century.

Close-up view of the handle construction of the four pronged pitchfork.

The hay rake had many small wooden teeth. These teeth broke often and had to be replaced. This tool cuts uniform teeth by driving a rough-cut piece of wood through the cutter with a wood mallet.

Every farm had an apple orchard. Shown here are two examples of the type of tool that would be used to pick the apple out of the tree. This type of apple picker would have been used throughout the eighteenth and early nineteenth centuries.

A wooden screw from an eighteenth century apple cider press. This screw is 8" in diameter and 5 feet long. This is only a portion of the screw and the screw was just a portion of the press. The screw was used to exert the pressure to squeeze the pulp, thus making cider.

Miniature plow, originally in the *Sorber Collection*. This is possibly a child's toy or a salesman's sample. Plow measures 14" long and 11" high.

Dibbles were used to poke a hole in the ground so that a seed could be planted. They came in all shapes, sizes, and materials.

On the farm, a cow chain would hold a cow in the stall as it was being milked. The branding iron was used to mark cattle and horses for identification. Both of these were hand-forged by a blacksmith. The cow chain shows very fine smith work.

Cow collar. This is probably eighteenth century European, but items like this would have been brought over to this country. The idea of the collar was to have the name of the owner engraved into the brass plaque, and if the cow was found roaming it could be returned to its proper owner.

A farmer's well was his source of water. To get water out of the well required a bucket. This bucket is 13" tall and 9" in diameter.

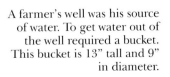

Butchering time was a special time on the farm and it required certain tools. This meat cleaver has the date 1831 punched into the iron.

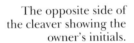

The opposite side of the cleaver showing the owner's initials.

Large, decorated, vegetable chopper. Because of the weight, this tool was designed to be rocked back and forth to do the cutting. The original wood guard is still with the chopper and that is a good thing, as the blade is still very sharp.

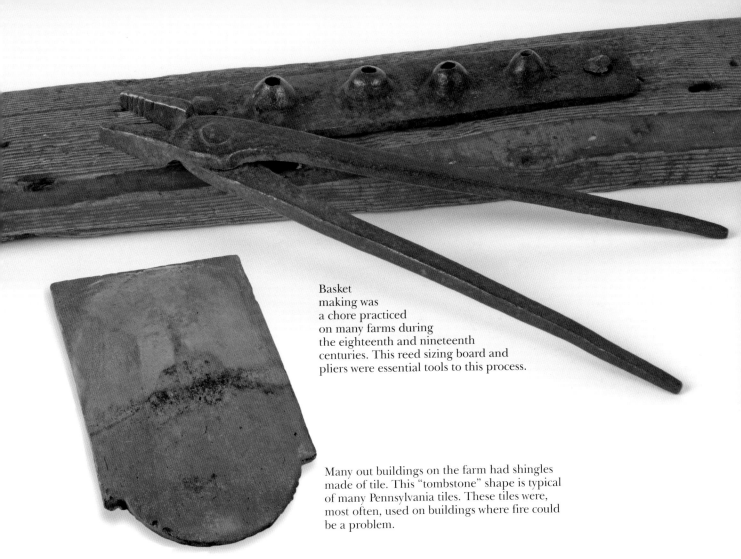

Basket
making was
a chore practiced
on many farms during
the eighteenth and nineteenth
centuries. This reed sizing board and
pliers were essential tools to this process.

Many out buildings on the farm had shingles
made of tile. This "tombstone" shape is typical
of many Pennsylvania tiles. These tiles were,
most often, used on buildings where fire could
be a problem.

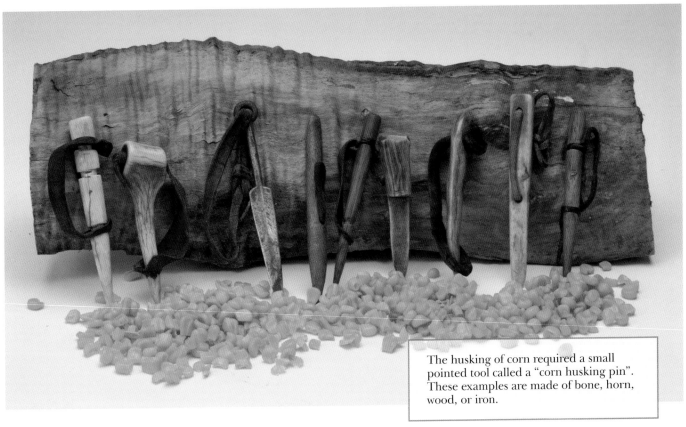

The husking of corn required a small
pointed tool called a "corn husking pin".
These examples are made of bone, horn,
wood, or iron.

Grain was often stored in large barrels made out of large tree trunks. This barrel is a hollowed sycamore log with a wood base inserted.

The spring house would house all items that needed refrigeration. Shown here are two butter making tools, the piggin (a dipper), and the butter tub. Note the rusted bands on the tub, which would have come from being in water for so much of its life.

Rye winnowing basket used to separate the chaff from the grain. *Courtesy of Diane Hogg.*

Many early farms had small blacksmith facilities set up in one of the outbuildings. Nails were always needed. Pictured here are two nail headers and a handful of hand forged nails. The header worked like this. After being pointed by the smith a hot nail rod was put into the header, the portion of the rod protruding from the top of the header would be struck four times, mushrooming the iron rod, and producing what is known as a rose head nail.

The turf axe was a necessary farm tool for digging out stumps and creating drainage ditches.

The holtzaxe, or splitting axe, was another tool crucial to the early farm, as firewood was always in steady demand all year long.

Another form of the turf axe. These axes were always a lighter form of axe than the felling or splitting axe.

Eighteenth century hewing hatchet with smith's markings.

Hewing hatchet with a leather guard. The guard is new, but it was copied from an original.

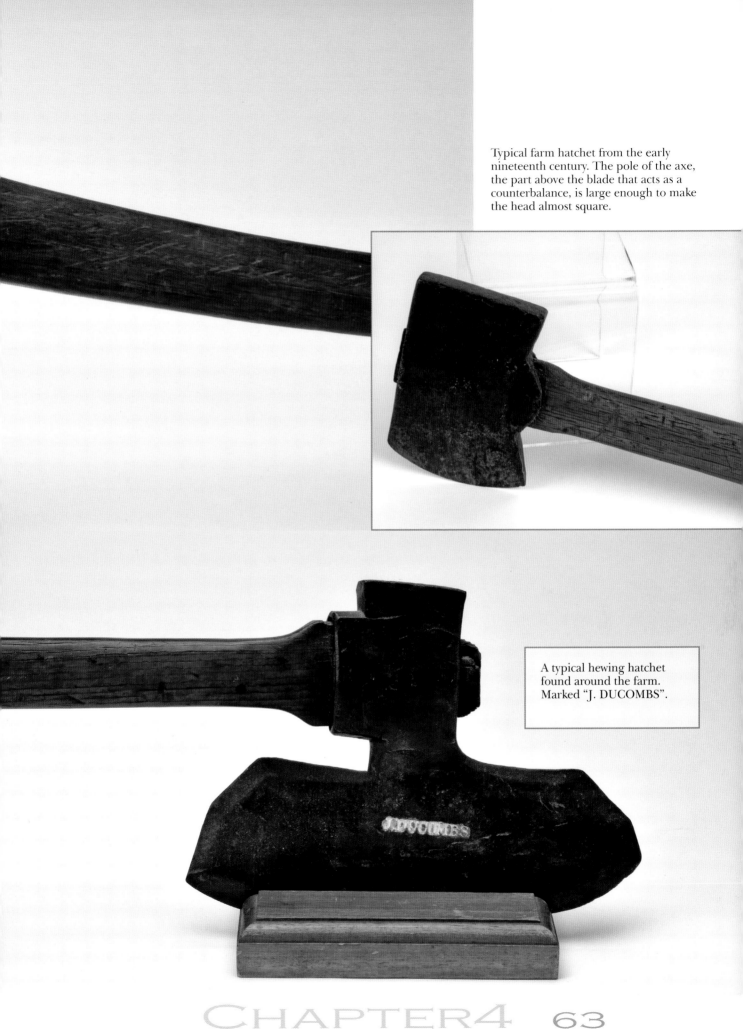

Typical farm hatchet from the early nineteenth century. The pole of the axe, the part above the blade that acts as a counterbalance, is large enough to make the head almost square.

A typical hewing hatchet found around the farm. Marked "J. DUCOMBS".

Will be exposed to Sale,

By Public Vendue,

On *Seventh* day the *Tenth* Instant,

AT 10 O'CLOCK, A. M.

On the premises of Job Cowperthwaite, situate in Chester township, on the road leading from Moorestown to Haddonfield, about two miles from the former and four from the latter, near Friends' Brick School House on said road,

ALL THE

TIMBER TREES

Upon the said premises, containing about 11 acres, among which are valuable Chesnut, Locust, Poplar, Oak, and other Trees, suitable for saw logs, rails, posts, cordwood, &c. A further description is deemed unnecessary. The premises will be run out in lots to suit purchasers, and the conditions be made known at the sale. Any person wishing to view the property may apply to Job Cowperthwaite, living on the premises, or to either of us.

BENJAMIN HUNT,
ASA MATLACK.

2d Mo. 1st. 1821.

Printed by P. M. Lafourcade, N. W. corner of Second & Race Streets, Philadelphia.

Timber made many farms quite valuable. This broadside describes timber between Moorestown and Haddonfield, New Jersey, which was to be auctioned off in 1821.

Practically every farm had a pond and during the winter months ice skating was a favorite sport with adults and children alike. These early nineteenth century ice skates are examples of some of the types used.

64

Public Sale.

ON SATURDAY, FEBRUARY 16, 1850, AT 1 O'CLOCK, P. M.,

Will be offered at public sale at the residence of the subscriber in Rapho township, Lancaster county, on the public road leading from Manheim to Groff's Fulling mill, about 2 miles from the former place, 1 mile from Gantz's tavern, and the same distance from Deeg's tavern, the following valuable personal property, viz.:

1 Milch Cow,
SHOATES,
HAY BY THE TON,

A Bureau, a Kitchen-dresser Beds & Bedsteads, 2 Dining Tables, a Cupboard Chairs, a Woodstove and Pipe, Iron Kettles, Iron Pots, Pans, Tubs, Barrels, together with a great variety of other articles not enumerated.

Attendance will be given, and terms of sale made known on said day, by

JACOB SMITH.

February, 2, 1850.

D. BARD ROCK, Printer, "Planet" Office, Manheim, Pa.

There were times when farms had to be sold. This broadside advertises such a sale in February 1850.

CHAPTER5
Transportation and the Conestoga Wagon

The Conestoga wagon was developed in southeastern Pennsylvania sometime before 1716. That was the year of the first written record of the wagon, and it was then listed as the "Conestogoe Waggon."

This vehicle was not one for personal travel; it was the tractor trailer of the day. Its only purpose was to haul merchandise from one place to another. There was no provision made for riders in the wagon; there were no seats. The driver or teamster either walked, rode the near wheel horse, as seen in the photo, or sat on the "lazy board." This was a board that slid out from under the wagon body on the left side of the wagon so that someone could sit or stand on it to regulate the brake lever, when the brake was needed. The horses were controlled by the teamster who had control of the "jerk line," which was a single rein connected to the lead animal.

Following the Revolutionary War, with improved roads, larger wagons began to appear. These wagons would haul goods over the entire developed country. They could haul as much as 100 hundred weight, or 10,000 pounds of freight. They carried farm produce to markets, they traveled to the mills, and they carried merchandise over the mountains to West Virginia and beyond. Many of the roads that started out simply as lanes eventually became turnpikes, and the highway system that we know today was begun. For nearly thirty years, following the War of 1812, this wagon was "king of the road." As time progressed, railroads and canals became the important modes of transportation and the Conestoga wagon slowly faded into history.

The Hager Store received merchandise in Conestoga Wagons ninety years ago.

THE HAGER STORE received merchandise in Conestoga Wagons ninety years ago.

The Conestoga wagon was the most important vehicle in use during the eighteenth and nineteenth centuries here in America. It was the tractor-trailer of its day, and no passengers ever rode in this vehicle. It was strictly used for carrying freight with the teamster riding the "near side" wheel horse, the horse nearest the front wheel.

Scale model, 1" = 1', of the Conestoga wagon made by the author. Every item on the real wagon is incorporated into this model.

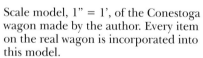

Another view showing the tool box side of the wagon.

Boots used by the teamster along with an original tool box lid with the usual ornate iron work for the hinges and hasp.

The grease bucket held the "grease" used to lubricate the axles and hubs and it hung under the bed of the wagon at the rear. This lubricant was a mixture of pine tar and grease, and in many of the old buckets the smell of pine tar is still strong. Tradition has the six-horse team wearing bells with the wheel team wearing three bells, the middle team wearing four bells and the lead team wearing five bells. Quite often the horse the teamster rode, the wheel horse, carried no bells.

The wagon jack. This jack is dated 1799. When it was necessary to lubricate the wheels and axles, the jack was placed under the axle and the wagon jacked up just enough to raise the massive wheel off of the ground. The linch pin was removed from the axle, the wheel pulled slightly off the axle, and grease added. Then it was all put back together. This process would have been done several times during a trip, such as, one from Lancaster, Pennsylvania, to Philadelphia.

The rough lock was a short section of heavy chain that was locked around the rim of the wheel at the point where the wheel touches the road. It was used when the wagon was on a long slope down a hill with the brake on and the rear wheels not turning. With this happening, but the wagon still moving, this chain prevented a flat spot being worn on the iron tire. Many rough locks have links that are worn paper thin from being scraped on the road. The wooden rough lock is a whimsy carved from one piece of wood, which could very well have been made by an old teamster who in his youth used many of them.

The iron work found on the Conestoga Wagon is very collectable. The blacksmith working on the wagon had the chance to show off his skill of forging the soft iron into artistic shapes and sizes. Two stay chain hooks, double tree hasp, and a hub cap are examples of the skill of that blacksmith. The bells were mounted into the hames of the lead team of horses.

A rear bolster pin and examples of the very intricately linked chain used with the Conestoga Wagon. Because of the weight of the wagons when loaded, the chain had to be able to stand tremendous stress. This method of interlocking multiple links made that strength possible, as several links would have to break before the chain would snap.

A rear hound plate and double tree spreader with the fifth chain attached. Notice how tight the linkage is on the spreader chain.

Other iron pieces found on the Conestoga are the front hound band, dated 1716, and the double tree hammer. The hoof knife, with leather sheath, and brass knuckles belonged to the teamster. And the forged horse bit is typical of that used on the teams.

This hames, with the two staples attached, belonged to a Conestoga team. These staples held one side of the set of bells. This is one-half of the total hames, the other piece of wood being a mirror image.

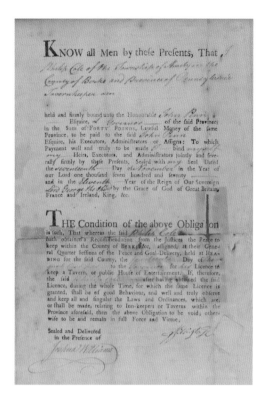

Typical sign seen hanging from the tavern. This particular building is located in western Pennsylvania and is part of the collection of log buildings in Old Bedford Village, Bedford, Pennsylvania.

Being on the road for long periods of time made the tavern and wagon stand a very vital part of the teamsters life. This Berks County, Pennsylvania, tavern license is dated 1770.

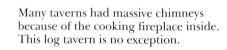

Many taverns had massive chimneys because of the cooking fireplace inside. This log tavern is no exception.

Inside the wagon stand or tavern, the teamster would find refreshment after a long, hard day on the road. These bottles represent the type of bottles that would be found at the bar from the 1600s through the early 1800s. The pewter plates were very common at taverns during this time, and the glass is a typical late 1700s wine glass.

Along with the bottles, the teamster would be familiar with mugs, wooden tankards, gaming chips and dice, long stemmed pipes, and ale shoes. This "shoe" was used to heat the ale by pushing the toe end of the shoe into warm coals, or sitting it on top of a cast iron stove. When the ale was warm, it would be poured into a glass or mug.

The Conestoga Wagon traveled the roads to such an extent that small roads became major highways. The mill was a major stop for these wagons as they picked up their barrels of grain to be transported to the storeowner. The millstone is 20" in diameter and 2" thick. Along with the stone is a grain sack marked "JOHN GOOD No.6 1836", a grain bag marker for "NATHANEL MERKY," and a barrel brand that reads "C.H. SNYDER SUPERFINE".

Mile markers were common along many of the major roadways. This marker, dated 1771, tells the teamster that he is thirty-seven miles from Philadelphia.

A favorite story told about the teamster is that when hauling kegs of liquor, the teamster would always carry a small gimlet. When the timing was right he would slide up one of the barrel bands, and with the gimlet drill a very small hole into the barrel where the band had been. He could then remove the amount of drink he chose, plug the hole with a small sliver of wood, and slide the band down into the proper position. Nobody would ever know. Shown here are four small gimlets of the type that would have been used to do the deed.

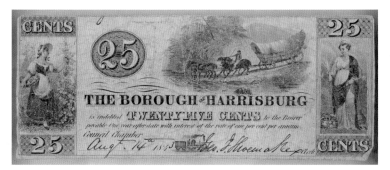

The Conestoga Wagon was so important to the nation that pictures of it found their way onto the currency of the day.

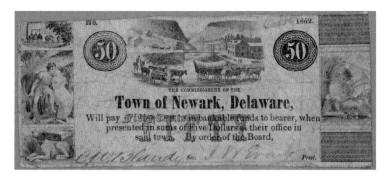

The importance of transportation and the Conestoga wagon during the eighteenth and nineteenth centuries was enormous. Turnpikes had to be built to support the large amount of wagon traffic, as the smaller roads were constantly clogged. To finance these turnpikes, money was borrowed and receipts given. The "Chambersburg & Bedford Turnpike Road Company" issued this receipt in 1818.

In 1862, even the small town of Newark, Delaware, found time to place a Conestoga Wagon on one of their local notes.

CHAPTER 6
The Blacksmith

T he eighteenth century blacksmith shop was, give or take, about 28' x 32' in size with a dirt floor, pitched roof, and of masonry or framed construction. The main structure in the shop was the forge. The air for the forge was supplied by a large wooden bellows, generally 3-4 feet across, which was pumped by the smith. The anvil was located next to the forge, with its height from the floor being "knuckle high" for the smith. Next to the anvil was a tub of water for quenching and cooling the finished iron product. With this simple equipment and a supply of charcoal and bar iron, the smith would create magic.

Any item made of iron, unless it was cast, was made by the blacksmith. The tools that were brought with the first colonists to these shores were made by the smiths of their homelands. Because of their importance, it did not take long for smiths to set up shop in America and begin producing the necessary implements required for the farm, especially nails and horseshoes. As time went on the smiths would create many of the household utensils used in the kitchen, along with lighting devices, locks and keys, door hinges, and the vast amount of ornamental iron found on the Conestoga wagon. The blacksmith was indispensable to the lives of the early colonists and because of this he often held a very prominent position in the community.

The following photographs illustrate many artifacts created by the eighteenth and early nineteenth century blacksmith and the tools he used to create them.

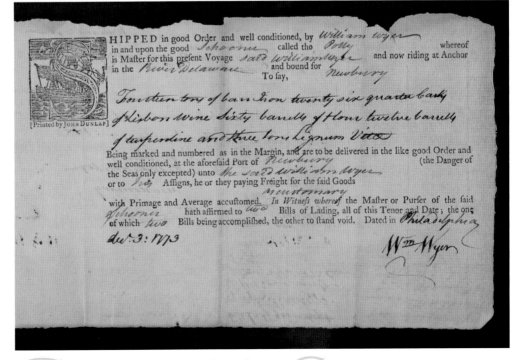

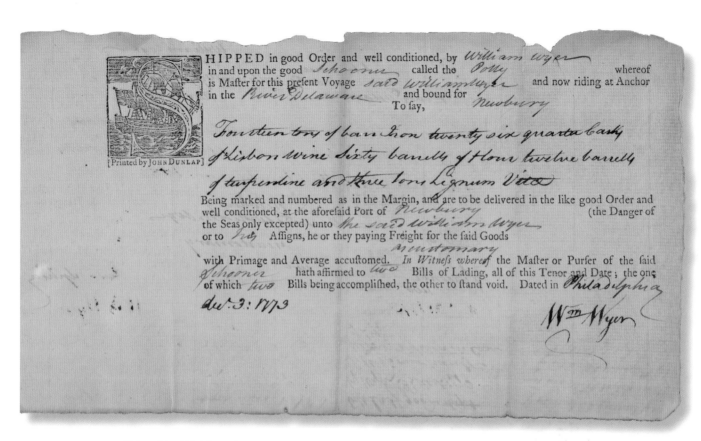

SHIPPED in good Order and well conditioned, by *William Wyer* in and upon the good *Schooner* called the *Polly* whereof is Master for this present Voyage *said William Wyer* and now riding at Anchor in the *River Delaware* and bound for *Newbury* To say,

Fourteen tons of bar Iron twenty six quarter casks of Lisbon wine sixty barrells of Flour twelve barrells of turpentine and three tons Lignum Vitæ

Being marked and numbered as in the Margin, and are to be delivered in the like good Order and well conditioned, at the aforesaid Port of *Newbury* (the Danger of the Seas only excepted) unto *the said William Wyer* or to *his* Assigns, he or they paying Freight for the said Goods *accustomary* with Primage and Average accustomed. *In Witness whereof* the Master or Purser of the said *Schooner* hath affirmed to *two* Bills of Lading, all of this Tenor and Date; the one of which *two* Bills being accomplished, the other to stand void. Dated in *Philadelphia*

Decr 3: 1773

Wm Wyer

[Printed by JOHN DUNLAP]

Printed in 1773 by John Dunlap, the first printer to print the Declaration of Independence, this Bill of Lading lists fourteen tons of bar iron, twenty six quarter casks of Lisbon wine, sixty barrels of flour, twelve barrels of turpentine, and three tons of lignum vitae wood. Bar iron was the mainstay material that the blacksmith used in his trade. When heated in a forge, it could be shaped into many useful implements such as cooking utensils, iron tools of all kinds, plows, rakes, and the ornamental iron used on the Conestoga Wagon … the list goes on.

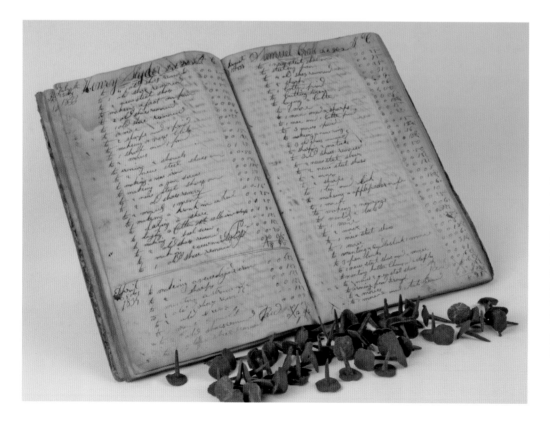

Blacksmith's day book. This is a listing of all of the work done by the blacksmith in the year 1833. The listings include making gun screws, making a new leg for a pan, mending a candlestick, ironing a wagon, making an apple peeler knife, ironing a wagon feed box, etc. Pictured also are a group of smith made bellow's nails. These are the nails that held the leather to the large forge bellows.

Anvils made before 1800 are often called Colonial anvils. In an English directory of 1787, Samuel Alsop is listed as being an anvil, vise, and screw maker. This anvil does not have the horn so common to the anvils made later, so it is safe to assume that this anvil was made very early in his career. The weight of an anvil is designated by three numbers on the side of the anvil. The first number is in "hundredweight" which equals 112 pounds, the second number is one quarter of the 112 pounds, and the third number is simply in pounds. Add them up and you get the approximate weight of the anvil. The weight of the Alsop anvil is 92 pounds.

Small stump anvil dated 1775. The anvil was mounted into a stump and used for lighter work. The face measures 1.75" x 6.25".

Another Colonial anvil with traces of original red paint. This one has the early horn, which indicates a slightly later date, but still in the eighteenth century.

The swage block was a blacksmith tool that enabled the smith to shape hot metal to an exact shape. This swage block was used to shape ladle bowls, spoon bowls, and funnels. The top right corner of the block has a small piece broken out but it would still be useable. Next to the block is a fine example of the smith's art. This Moravian door latch has a removable handle. The latch itself did not actually lock, but if the handle was removed there was no way to enter, thus the door was "locked."

For rough work, the striking sledge was used by the smith's helper. The finer work was executed by the blacksmith, with the heavy pounding done by the helper, both working together. Also pictured, a rain gutter support, horse tie, two butterfly hinges, and two pair of pliers are just a few examples of the work done by the smith.

A larger stump anvil used in the shop. This one is dated 1818.

The solid cone mandrel was used when forming round objects that required a slight taper. It was used when making bands for the hubs of wheels on wagons, which required such a taper.

When making certain shapes, a top and bottom fuller were required. This example would have been used in making the knob end of fireplace tongs, or similar objects. The bottom fuller was set into the hole of the anvil and the top fuller was held by the blacksmith and hit with a hammer. Each tool formed half of the shape required.

Every town had a pump near the center square so that travelers could water their horses and refresh themselves. These pumps had a long iron handle that needed to be pumped to bring the water up to the surface. This blacksmith made handle has the smith's initials and the date, 1800.

Hatchet: c. 1820
"I think Jonas is ready for his own hatchet now. Tomorrow I'll take the waggon into town and stop at the Blacksmiths."

A very small early nineteenth century hatchet with the original handle.

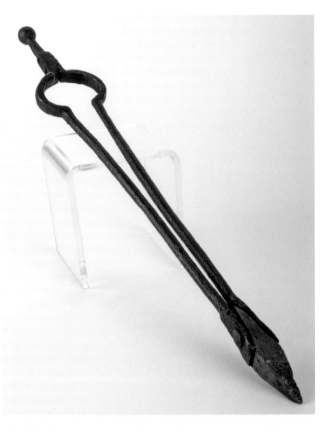

A blacksmith made "charcoal" rake. Huge stacks of wood were used in the making of charcoal for the blacksmith. After the wood was turned into charcoal the very hot coals had to be raked out into thin layers so they could cool. The extension on the socket of this rake would keep the wood handle far enough away from the intense heat to keep it from burning.

The blacksmith often made one thing out of something else. In this case, fireplace tongs were converted into a soldering copper, a tool used to solder tin.

Two very fine examples of the art created by the smith. Both are eighteenth century door latches.

The twitch was a tool used to quiet a high spirited horse while having its shoes replaced. The twitch was placed over the lip of the animal and pressure was slowly applied by adjusting the twitch tighter. The pressure applied to the upper lip from the twitch releases endorphins, which increased the tolerance to unpleasant procedures. Both of these items are smith made.

Two barrel locks and keys, both blacksmith made.

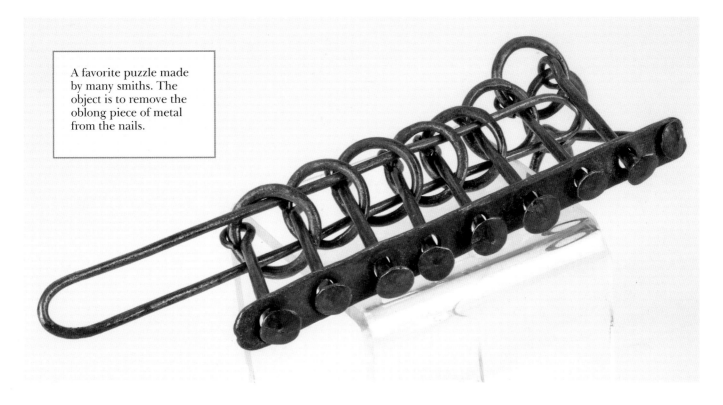

A favorite puzzle made by many smiths. The object is to remove the oblong piece of metal from the nails.

The two stirrups and the side saddle stirrup are examples of the skill of many smiths. The wagon pin in the shape of a horse head took considerable skill with hammer, chisel, and forge.

Hinge making was another job of the smith. These examples are characteristic of when art and pure function meet.

The kitchen was still another area where the blacksmith was indispensable. All cooking utensils were either cast or forged; the spider, toaster, and broiler shown here are typical examples of his skill.

Some of the many shapes and sizes of the early strap hinge.

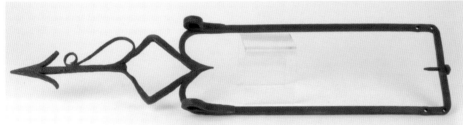

Although not complete this weathervane is another example of the diversity of the smith's skills. Most likely this vane flew over a gristmill in its heyday. It measures 7.5" x 32.5".

A set of sled runners for a child's sled.

The tools of the blacksmith were fairly simple. Some of the most common tools used were the coal shovel, used to add charcoal to the forge, the poker, used to move coals around in the forge, and the hammers used to shape the hot iron. Along with the tools already mentioned in this chapter, the smith would create works of art that are lasting to this day.

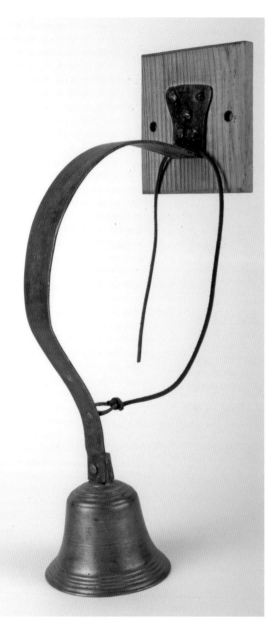

Shop keeper's bell. The bell would be mounted on the inside wall of the shop and the leather thong would go through the wall so that the customer on the outside could ring the bell.

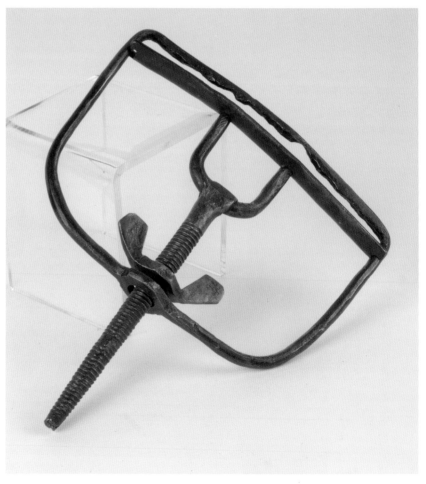

A unique blacksmith made mop head for the industrious person of the home.

Every once in a while a craftsman would create a whimsy of his or her work. The following miniature tools and utensils were made by an unknown blacksmith sometime during the mid- to late nineteenth century. There is some conjecture as to why these were made. Some think that they were made for children while others feel that they were made to show off the skill of the smith. No matter why they were originally made they are here today to be enjoyed for the simple reason that they are unique. This miniature 3-inch "spider" pan is the first example in this group of miniatures.

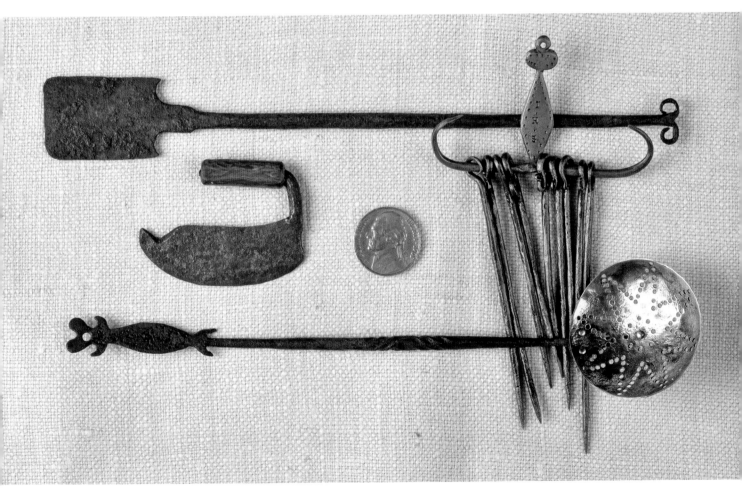

From top to bottom: Oven peel, 7.75 inches; food chopper, 2 inches; skewer holder with skewers, 2.75 inches wide; skimming ladle, dated 1824, 7.5 inches.

Above:
Top to bottom: Tailor's iron, 2.25 inches; meat fork, 6.5 inches; raft shackles (these were used to hold logs together as they were floated down river), 4.5 inches.

Below:
From top to bottom: Pitch fork, 10.5 inches; splitting wedge, 3 inches; hay knife, 4 inches; axe with large rattail wing nut that is actually threaded, 4.25 inches; hand auger, 4.25 inches; felling axe, 5.25 inches; hatchet, 3 inches; fire striker, 1 inch; claw hammer, 3.25 inches.

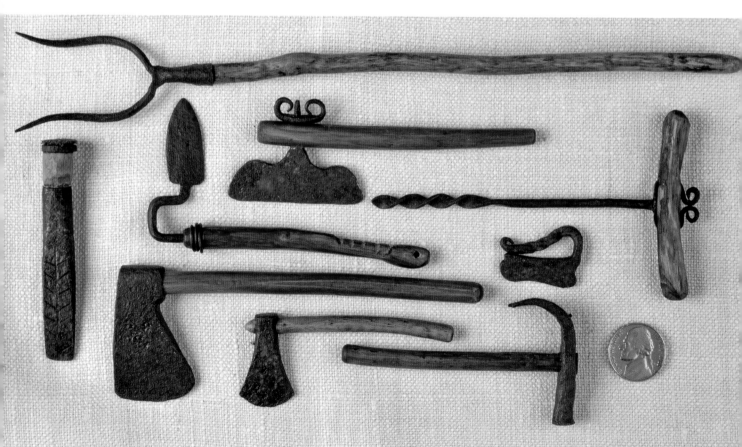

From left to right: Hanging ratchet candleholder, 7.5 inches; candleholder with turned wood base, 4 inches; hanging candleholder, 5 inches.

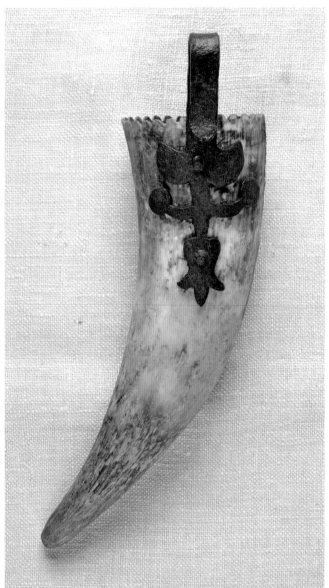

The hook on this whetstone horn, used to carry the sharpening stone for the sickle and scythe, is a fine example of the art that many blacksmiths were capable of producing.

CHAPTER 7
The Cabinetmaker

A typical cabinet shop of the eighteenth century probably looked like a modern day garage or shed. They were most often of frame construction with a pitched roof and wood floor. On the walls were crude wood shelves for holding tools. A wood turning lathe would be along one wall, a workbench would be along another wall, and there were probably tools and lumber hanging from the ceiling. Sometimes these shops had their own heat source, but many times they "borrowed" the heat from the cabinetmaker's home, which was frequently connected to the shop. They were simple affairs but the products that came out of them were often works of art.

The cabinetmaker's tools were basic but effective, and because of his apprenticeship training the cabinetmaker was able to create the chairs, tables, clocks, hutches, bowls, plates, storage boxes, and all of the material that the early colonist required. At first, many of the tools he used were made in England, but as time went on, the blacksmiths in America were able to equal the British blacksmith's skills and create many of the iron tools that the cabinetmaker required. Also, plane makers and other specialized tool makers began to appear in the colonies, and by the time of the Revolutionary War the cabinetmaker could have been using mostly American made tools.

Many books have been written about the colonial cabinetmaker and his trade. The following photographs give the reader a sense of some of the more unique, unusual, and common tools that were used. All of these artifacts found a home in the eighteenth century cabinet shop.

The eighteenth century cabinetmaker carried a number of tools in his chest, but the tool that he considered "king" was the wood working plane. Second from left, and the largest of the planes, is the crown-molding plane. This plane made the molding that attached to the corner between the wall and the ceiling in many homes. Because of the wide cut of this plane, (3.75") the friction between the blade and wood was tremendous, and for that reason it often required two men to do the job, one man to push and the other to pull. The hole at the front of the plane is where the handle for the second man would be placed. It was usually a dowel that could be inserted then; when the dowel was not needed, it was removed. The plane on the left and the one third from the left are panel-raising planes. They shaved the edges of panels on a bevel, making what is called a raised panel. The fourth plane is a narrower version of the crown molder.

The owner of this skew-mouthed rabbet plane thought enough of it to carve his initials into the side. The rabbet plane would cut a step into the long edge of a board in preparation for joining it to another board.

A curved, apple wood plane was used to smooth the top edges of barrels while the other planes are various shapes of the eighteenth century plow plane. The plow plane was used to make the groove in the tongue and groove boards that made up flooring in houses.

A Dutch rabbet plane with highly carved designs. As colonists from many countries arrived in America, many of them brought their own tools. The tools all worked alike, but each country's tool style had a slightly different look.

The adjustable arm plow plane was made by "E GERE, N. YORK", and the other plow plane was made by "J. STILES, 1807". The spill plane shown with the spills is the only plane whose main purpose was to make shavings, while with all other planes, the shavings were a by-product. These spills, or shavings, were used to move a fire from one place to another, in lieu of a match.

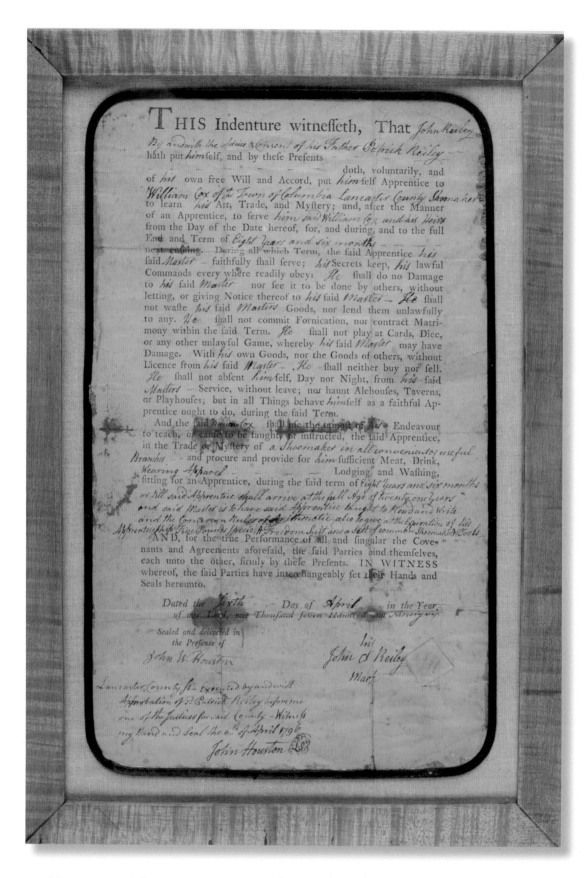

THIS Indenture witnesseth, That *John Reiley* By and with the Advice & Consent of his Father *Patrick Reiley* hath put *himself*, and by these Presents

doth, voluntarily, and of *his* own free Will and Accord, put *him* self Apprentice to *William Cox of the Town of Columbia Lancaster County Shoemaker* to learn *his* Art, Trade, and Mystery; and, after the Manner of an Apprentice, to serve *him said William Cox and his Heirs* from the Day of the Date hereof, for, and during, and to the full End and Term of *Eight Years and six months* next ensuing. During all which Term, the said Apprentice *his* said *Master* — faithfully shall serve; *his* Secrets keep, *his* lawful Commands every where readily obey: *He* shall do no Damage to *his* said *Master* nor see it to be done by others, without letting, or giving Notice thereof to *his* said *Master* — *He* shall not waste *his* said *Masters* Goods, nor lend them unlawfully to any. *He* shall not commit Fornication, nor contract Matrimony within the said Term. *He* shall not play at Cards, Dice, or any other unlawful Game, whereby *his said Master* may have Damage. With *his* own Goods, nor the Goods of others, without Licence from *his* said *Master* — *He* shall neither buy nor sell. *He* shall not absent *himself*, Day nor Night, from *his* said *Masters* — Service, without leave; nor haunt Alehouses, Taverns, or Playhouses; but in all Things behave *himself* as a faithful Apprentice ought to do, during the said Term.

And the said *William Cox* shall use the utmost of *his* Endeavour to teach, or cause to be taught, or instructed, the said Apprentice, in the Trade or Mystery of *a Shoemaker in all convenient or useful Branches* — and procure and provide for *him* sufficient Meat, Drink, *Wearing Apparel*, Lodging, and Washing, fitting for an Apprentice, during the said term of *Eight Years and six months or till said Apprentice shall arrive at the full Age of twenty one Years and said Master is to have said Apprentice taught to Read and Write and the Common Rules of Arithmetic also to give at the Expiration of his Apprenticeship Five Pounds Specie A Freedom Suit and a sett of common Shoemaker Tools*

AND, for the true Performance of all and singular the Covenants and Agreements aforesaid, the said Parties bind themselves, each unto the other, firmly by these Presents. IN WITNESS whereof, the said Parties have interchangeably set their Hands and Seals hereunto.

Dated the *Sixth* Day of *April* in the Year of our Lord, one Thousand seven Hundred and Ninety six

Sealed and delivered in the Presence of

John W. Houston

John ✗ Reiley
Mark

Lancaster County ss — Executed by and with Approbation of P. Patrick Reiley before me one of the Justices for said County — Witness my Hand and Seal the 6th of April 1796

John Houston

Many young people were sent to a master craftsman to learn the trade of that person. This process was called an apprenticeship, and the agreement usually lasted seven years. There was a contract drawn up between the parent and the craftsman, with the young person involved having very little to say about the whole event. This example, although not a cabinetmaker's but a shoemaker's, agreement states what must be done in order to keep everything legal. The Indenture, dated 1796, is giving John Reiley to William Cox, shoemaker, of Lancaster County, Pennsylvania, for eight years and six months to learn the trade. John Reiley signed his name with his "X". Wonder if he ever finished?

The cabinetmaker's glue pot. This acted as a double boiler with hot water in the larger pot and the glue in the smaller pot. To apply the glue, a small piece of wood was used.

Most cabinetmakers did many types of woodwork. Wheels and hubs were often made in small cabinet shops, if they had the equipment. Pictured are two hooked hub reamers and a wagon tire clamp. The reamer with no handle was made by "M SEIGER". After the straight hole in the hub was drilled, a reamer was used to give the hole a tapered surface. The hook on the reamer held a weight, which would help pull the reamer into the hub, as the turning was done by hand and was very difficult. The tire clamp held the iron tire in place on the rim as it was being attached to the wheel.

Other tools in the cabinet shop were the iron brace and bit for drilling holes, the traveler for measuring linear distances, and the hacksaw. The hacksaw is shown without a blade.

Certain tools were required to make chairs. The seat had to be hollowed out with a small hollowing adz, top left, and the scorp, lower left, would then be used to smooth the rough spots. For other projects the screwdriver, and the hand adz, top center, would be used. When mortise and tenon joints were made, the holes to join them were drilled slightly off center. Then the drift pins, right, when pushed into the assembled mortise and tenon joint holes, pulled the joints tightly together. When the drift pins were removed, the final wooden locking pin was tapped into place.

Chisels were an essential tool to any early cabinetmaker for making the smaller mortise and tenon joints in cabinetry. Keeping them sharp was an important job and that job often fell to the apprentice.

The dovetail saw and the back saw are both marked "I. V. HILL", "HOWEL", "LONDON". Also shown is a race knife for scribing numerals to joints so that the proper pieces are fit together, along with a crude hand clamp with a very large "rattail" wing nut. The eighteenth century cabinetmaker's square has lead and iron rivets holding the pieces together.

The bench "side rest" was used to keep smaller pieces of wood from sliding while they were being worked on. One end hooked to the edge of the workbench while the other supported the wood piece being worked. The strap hammers and pliers were found in every cabinet shop.

Other eighteenth century tools found in the shop. A marking gauge, made of bird's-eye maple, was used to lay out the lines for cutting a mortise. The keyhole saw cut tight diameters. The spoke shave was used for light finishing of wood. The two screw plates, made by Peter Stubs of Warrington, England, would thread the ends of fine iron rods. The plane float was used to file the inside of the throat of the plane when it was being made.

Bench "holdfasts" were used in the eighteenth century work benches to hold the wood being worked. There were holes in the bench for "holdfasts" to be placed, and with a tap from a hammer they held tight. To loosen them would require another tap of the hammer.

An eighteenth century panel saw, the grip being attached to the blade with lead rivets.

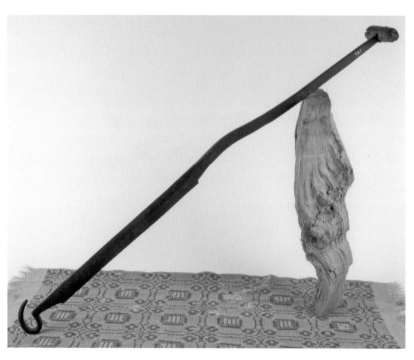

Block knife: This knife was hooked to a staple in a large stump and used to rough cut a piece of wood to shape. Once the rough shape was determined then the finer tools were used to finish the piece.

The pit saw was not a tool that the cabinetmaker would always have in his shop, but it was a tool that was needed to make his logs into planks. This job could have been done by the carpenter, or possibly, by the cabinetmaker himself. The process required two men, one on top of the log being sawn and one below. Sometimes this sawing was done with the bottom man in a pit, thus the name "pit saw," and sometimes it was done all above ground with the top man up on a large sawhorse. The lower handle, not shown, was a small wooden removable one. It was designed this way so that if the cut was not finished along the entire length of the log, the saw could be removed from the saw kerf.

To make both external and internal threads on a piece of wood, a threading block would be used. The external threads were cut with the block, which had a cutting blade inside, and the internal threads were cut with the iron tap. The wood handle to the tap is missing.

This cabinet maker purchased two boxes of 8 x 10 glass from "Samuel Wetherill & Son, Druggists, Oil and Colourmen" in 1814.

Many shops used veneer on their furniture and to make veneer a special saw was required. The wood to be cut into veneer was clamped vertically into a vice and two men would saw, very carefully, down the full length of the piece. Note the large "rattail" wing nut holding the blade taunt and the 3.75" wide blade.

Collectors often find that the hunt for artifacts is the most fun. Sometimes you find something, sometimes you don't. You have a subject matter in mind when you are hunting but all of a sudden you find that really "neat" piece that is of the right time period and the right price, but doesn't quite fit into the theme you are looking for. What do you do? Well, as you know, you buy it.

But, because of this "unpredictable" buying, all of a sudden there are many pieces in a collection that are quite unique but do not fit comfortably into the focus of that collection. The first seven chapters of this book follow that focus. This chapter called "Hodgepodge" contains the items that did not fit comfortably into the preceding chapters, but are still an important part of the life of Colonial America.

Eighteenth century garden rolling stone used to smooth out walkways after a rain. This practice of rolling walkways after a rain was common wherever gravel, shells, or even discarded and broken clay pipes were use as the walking surface. These rollers were made in both stone and iron, but seventeenth century English diarist John Evelyn felt that the best were made from ancient marble columns.

Typical continental currency in use during the Revolutionary War. Listing from top to bottom: the dates and states are as follows, 1776 New Jersey, 1776 Philadelphia, and 1774 Maryland.

The Revolutionary War was a traumatic event for the people living in America. Several reminders of this war are a blacksmith made iron fife, English horse pistol, and cannon ball found in 1954 on the Brandywine battlefield in Pennsylvania.

Paper currency common during the late eighteenth century. The dates on these bills are, from top to bottom, 1793, printed in France; 1773 Philadelphia; 1774 Maryland; and 1771 Philadelphia.

The wooden boot last is typical of the style of boot used during the Revolutionary War period. At this time, boots and shoes were made with no right or left foot shape, the idea being that as you wore the boot or shoe your feet would eventually form either the right or left fit. Ouch!

Mid-nineteenth century hitching post horse head used in Lancaster, Pennsylvania.

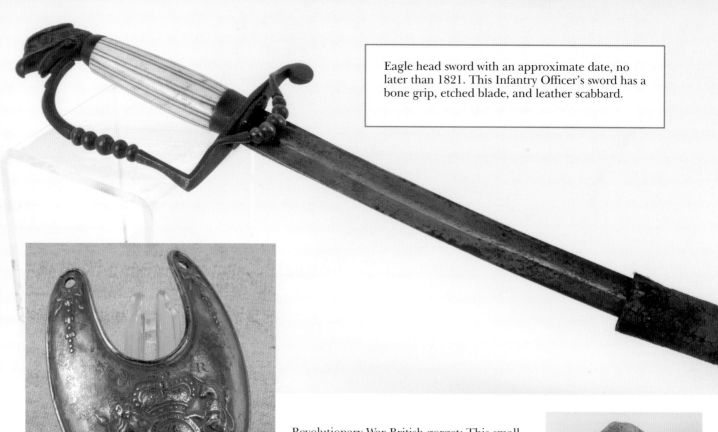

Eagle head sword with an approximate date, no later than 1821. This Infantry Officer's sword has a bone grip, etched blade, and leather scabbard.

Revolutionary War British gorget: This small item of officer's dress was the last remaining evidence of armor used in the military. It was worn around the neck as an indication of rank by commissioned officers. This gorget is silver plate over brass.

Die, made of hammered lead, found in New Jersey. It was a common practice for soldiers of the Revolutionary to hammer bullets into dice. The die measures .75" square.

Other Revolutionary War artifacts include a group of spurs, 12 pound cannon ball, two musket flints found on the Brandywine Battlefield, a "buck and ball" (buckshot and ball) paper cartridge, and a 69 caliber paper cartridge. Also shown are two pay vouchers dated 1781 and 1783. The smaller cannon ball is one half of what was called "chain shot." The powder, two balls, and the chain connecting them were loaded into a cannon. Often the force of the discharge caused the balls and chain to spin with such force that they broke apart before hitting the target. Notice the effect of the force of the shot by the twisted eyebolt in the ball.

A small eighteenth century drafting set with brass, ivory, and ebony
instruments. The case is covered with sharkskin.

Three seventeenth century
French playing cards.

Pewter button mold. The
molten pewter was poured
into the mold, then cooled.
The button design could
be changed by inserting a
different lead mold into the
wood holder. One button was
made at a time.

An eighteenth century stagecoach trunk. The name "I. Clifford, Phila" is marked in the lid with brass tacks, indicating that this round leather bound trunk saw much travel in and around Philadelphia.

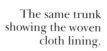

The same trunk showing the woven cloth lining.

Sampler made from an old bed sheet showing the stitching down the middle. To get a sheet wide enough for use on a bed, two pieces of woven cloth had to be sewn together. Anna Miller took her material from the center of the sheet. It is dated 1795. *From the collection of Diane Hogg.*

Wooden mold for making bricks. The raw clay was pressed into these molds, taken out while it was wet, and set aside to dry and await firing.

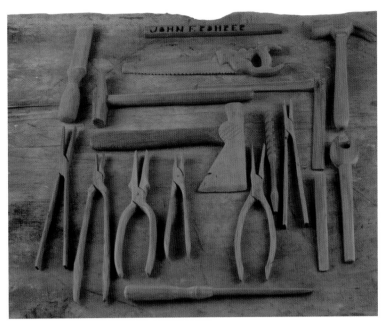

In many homes, old stove plates were used as protective backs for the fireplace. This stove plate, dated 1759, was originally the left side of a five plate stove known to collectors as the "I.A.R.B." plate. There is not much known about this stove plate and it is not known what the four initials represent. The plate's measurements are 22" x 24".

This set of tools was carved by John F. Rohrer sometime during the early twentieth century. He was born in 1856 and worked as a conductor for the Conestoga Traction Company in Lancaster, Pennsylvania. During that time he is known to have carved a large group of whimsies. The pliers are of interest as they pivot and are carved from a single piece of pine with only the pin added.

Wood box containing a small set of scales. Scales were used for a number of things including weighing medicines and hard currency. With the lack of a standard currency, being able to weigh the exact amount of gold and silver one had, or was to receive, was essential.

Another small scale, this one in a tin box with the original cloth lining. These were small enough that they could be carried very easily in a jacket pocket.

Bleeding patients by cutting a vein in the arm was a common practice used by doctors during the early years of this country. The procedure was to lance the vein, allowing the "bad" blood to flow out; thus enabling the patient to make new blood and recover from the illness. The vein was cut with a fleam, or lancet, shown here. Many historians believe that "bleeding" George Washington in 1799 was a major factor leading to his death.

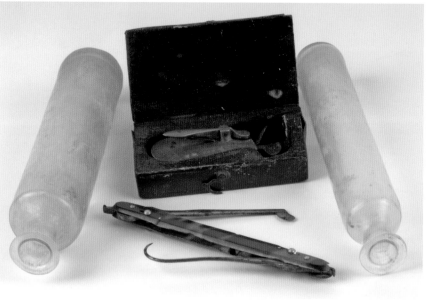

Two fleams, one with a tortoiseshell handle and the other cased. The cased fleam is marked "Wiegand and Snowden, Philadelphia". The case measures 1.5" x 2.75". The two glass bottles are eighteenth century medicine vials.

This tooth extractor would possibly keep many people from seeing the dentist. It would be hooked under the ailing tooth and twisted. Novocaine was nonexistent.

Mid- to late eighteenth century mold used to cast pewter spoons.

Philad^a June 27. 1826

Mr. Peter Bricker,

dr Sir

I regret to inform you that the enclosed notes has been endorsed by one of the Tellers of the Bank as counterfeit, probably you may recollect of having paid us among other notes, two Ten Dollar notes of this bank, after you where gone we examined the notes, finding a difference in these two notes we endorsed them with your name, as it is customery with us, a day two after having paid money to Tunis & Morris Merchants these two notes where among the rest, they where sent to bank by those Gentlemen and returned to us as counterfeit, we would have sent it on to you immediately, but did not know where to direct the letter, you will find enclosed a bill for the 2 Kegs Tobacco, and receipts for the Twenty Dollar received by the bearer

Very respectfully yours &c

Bartholomew & Blumner

Counterfeit money was a problem for Peter Bricker in 1826. Mr. Bricker was a merchant in Lancaster County, Pennsylvania, and this letter is informing him that Bartholomew and Blumner, the merchant he had recently purchased items from, would like to be reimbursed for the two, ten dollar counterfeit notes he gave them. They are also sending Bricker a bill for the two kegs of tobacco he received.

U.S. Patent Office model for a new way to cover a cured ham. This model, made by the inventor C. Van Vlec, is a carved wooden ham with the "new covering" now flaking off. The tag reads, "Resinous Compound for Covering Hams, June 30th 1857." The patent number for this item is #17709.

This seventeenth century bowling pin is not of American origin, but pins like this were used in this country. This pin was excavated in Amsterdam, Holland, is 6" tall and 1.25" in diameter. Because of the pin's size, it is assumed that it was used for table bowling.

When purchasing an item, change was given by cutting coins into "quarters" and "halves." These silver quarters and halves are all seventeenth and eighteenth century coins that were excavated in England. The large coin in the center still has a readable date, 1619. Coins similar to these were also used in the early colonies since the colonies did not have any local currency of their own.

The redware "thunder mug" or bedpan, on the left, was a very common item in every household. The other redware bowl is a utility item, used in the early kitchen for almost anything. This unglazed bowl was found beneath one of the streets in the city of Lancaster, Pennsylvania, during recent construction.

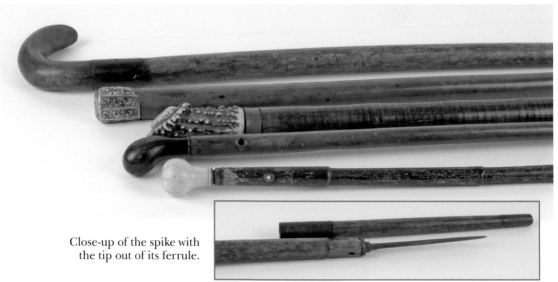

Typical walking canes of the eighteenth and early nineteenth centuries. The cane at the top of the photo has a spike hidden in the ferrule.

Close-up of the spike with the tip out of its ferrule.

These are items that every kitchen and tavern would have for preparing food. Pictured (clockwise) is a cast iron kettle, three legged pot made out of bell metal, copper tea kettle, wood and pewter funnel, pot lifter, potato rake for moving items around in the coals, and two iron trivets.

Grist mill wood gear measuring 18" in diameter and 4" thick. The teeth are 3" long.

An 1806 reward poster for a Swiss family, assumed to be indentured servants. It gives a very detailed description of the family who disappeared from the Delaware Paper Mills, Wilmington, Delaware.

Lead tokens known as "Abbot's money": The name is derived from the use of lead tokens by early fifteenth century English monasteries to pay laborers for their service. Later, any employer gave these tokens to his workers, and when the worker earned enough, they could be exchanged for real money. Each employer would have his individual design cast into them. There is not a date on the tokens shown, but they are, most likely, from the time period of 1700-1775. Although these were found in England, some tokens like these have shown up in Virginia.

Full sheet of uncut and unused vouchers to be paid by the Lancaster Cotton House in Lancaster, Pennsylvania. They were to be used between 1810 and 1819.

Delaware state lottery ticket dated 1836.

Litiz July 4th 1827

Mr David Bricker

Sir our Lodge Meets every full Moon at Six oClock in the afternoon only when full Moon Comes on Sunday then it meets on Monday following if therefore you wish to Com to this Meeting you will please to Com on Monday evening next

Your friend

Martin Manderbach

In 1827, Martin Manderbach invited David Bricker to a Masonic Lodge meeting in Lititz, Pennsylvania. This letter was folded to make its own envelope and then sealed with wax.

Taufschein, or baptismal certificate, printed in Ephrata, Pennsylvania, by G. Baumann.

Continental currency printed in Philadelphia by Hall and Sellers with dates (from left) of 1773, 1775, and 1775.

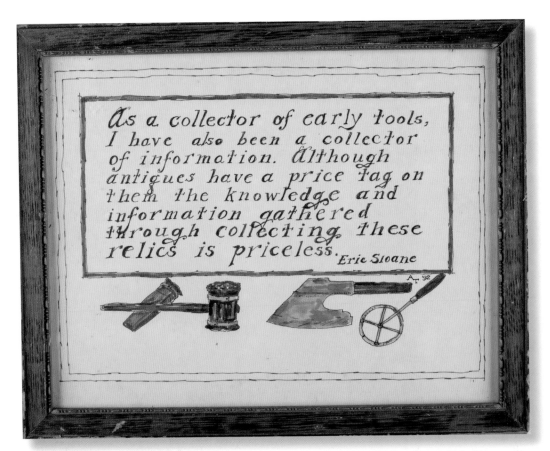

A statement by the famous author, painter, and philosopher of early Americana, Eric Sloane.